Improve your scales!

A workbook for examinations

Piano Grade 4

Paul Harris

Contents

Introduction   2
A♭ major   4
D♭ major   6
B major revision   8
B♭ major revision   9
E♭ major revision   10
C♯ minor   11
G♯ minor   14
F minor   17
C minor revision   20
Arpeggio exercises   21
Chromatic scale studies   22
Contrary motion scale studies   23
Performance tips   24
Scales   25
Arpeggios   29
Broken chords   30

© 2000 by Faber Music Ltd
First published in 1995 by Faber Music Ltd
Revised impression 2000
3 Queen Square London WC1N 3AU
Music and text typeset by Silverfen
Printed in England by Caligraving Ltd
All rights reserved

ISBN 0-571-51599-1

To buy Faber Music publications or to find out about the full range of titles available
please contact your local music retailer or Faber Music sales enquiries:

Faber Music Limited, Burnt Mill, Elizabeth Way, Harlow, CM20 2HX England
Tel: +44 (0)1279 82 89 82   Fax: +44 (0)1279 82 89 83
sales@fabermusic.com   www.fabermusic.com

Faber *ff* MUSIC

Introduction

To the student

Have you ever realised that it is much easier to learn something if you want to? Do you ever forget your telephone number? How many characters can you name from your favourite 'soap' or football team? Scales are not difficult to learn if you really want to learn them. Not only will they improve many aspects of your technique, but you will also get high marks in the scale section of grade exams, you will be able to learn pieces more quickly (difficult passages are often nothing more than scale patterns) and your sight-reading will improve too. Treat scales as friends – they will pay you great dividends!

To the teacher

Scales and arpeggios are often a real stumbling block for exam candidates and budding musicians. *Improve your scales!* is designed to make scale preparation and learning fun! Working through the book will encourage your pupils to approach scales and arpeggios methodically and thoughtfully. It will help with memory problems and turn scale-learning into an enjoyable experience.

The keys which also occur in *Improve your scales! Piano Grade 3* are presented here in revision format. Please refer to the earlier book for further useful practice material.

Simultaneous learning
Scales, sight-reading and aural are often the aspects of teaching relegated to the final few minutes of a lesson. The link between scales (particularly in the development of 'key-sense' and the recognition of melodic/harmonic patterns) and sight-reading is obvious, and there are many ways to integrate aural into the process too. Thus the use of the material in this book as a more central feature of a lesson is strongly recommended, especially when used in conjunction with *Improve your sight-reading!* Pupils will learn to become more musically aware, make fewer mistakes and allow the teacher to concentrate on teaching the music!

Using this book

The purpose of this workbook is to incorporate regular scale playing into lessons and daily practice, and to help pupils prepare for grade examinations. New scales are introduced throughout the book, in line with the grade 4 requirements of the Associated Board. You need not work at all sections, nor in the order as set out, but the best results may well be achieved by adhering fairly closely to the material.

Know the Notes! is to prove that the actual notes *are* known! Students should be encouraged to say the notes up and down until this can be done *really* fluently.

The **Finger Fitness** exercises are to strengthen the fingers and to cover technically tricky areas. To get the most out of the **Finger Fitness** exercises, the following practice method is recommended:

1 Practise each hand separately until you are really fluent. Then;

2 Practise the exercise hands together, repeating many times until you are confident of the fingering and can play it both fluently and evenly. That's *real* **Finger Fitness**!

When they are fluent you may like to add dynamic levels and alter the rhythm patterns.

The **Key pieces** place the material in a more musical context.

Have a go is to encourage thought 'in the key', through the improvisation or composition of a short tune.

As a further exercise to develop the ability to think in a key, encourage pupils to play (by ear) a well-known melody – for example, Happy Birthday or the National Anthem (major), 'Greensleeves' or 'God rest ye merry, gentlemen' (minor). You might like to ask pupils to improvise a simple variation on their chosen melody. This could be rhythmic or dynamic to begin. As they grow in confidence they might try 'decorating' the melody.

Say → **think** → **play!** is where the student finally plays the scale and arpeggio. The following method should really help the student memorise each scale and arpeggio:

1 **Say** the notes out loud, up and down, and repeat until fluent.

2 **Think** the notes and play the scale/arpeggio slowly.

3 **Play** the scale/arpeggio more fluently. By this time there should be no doubt in the performer's mind and there should certainly be no fumbles or wrong notes!

Marking

A marking system has been included to help you and the student monitor progress and to act as a means of encouragement. It is suggested that you adopt a grading system as follows:

A   Excellent work!

B   Good work, but keep at it!

C   A little more practice would be a good idea!

D   No time to lose – get practising at once!

Revision

At the end of each stage you will find a **Revision Practice** table. As the new scales become more familiar you will wish your student to revise them regularly. This table is to encourage a methodical approach to scale practice, and to show that there are endless ways of practising scales and arpeggios! Fill out the table for each week, or each practice session, as follows:

1   Choose a different rhythmic pattern each time from the following:

2   Choose a different dynamic level.

As students get into the habit of good scale and arpeggio practice they should no longer need the table.

Articulation

Initially, practise and play all scales and arpeggios *legato*. Once they are really secure, they can also be practised and played *staccato*.

Fingering

The suggested fingerings throughout the book are appropriate for the preparation of scales and arpeggios for examination purposes, but need not necessarily be followed strictly.

Group teaching

Improve your scales! is ideal for group teaching. Members of the group should be asked to comment on performances of the **Finger Fitness** exercises – was the tone even? Were the fingers moving rhythmically and together when necessary? Was the pulse even? *etc.* The **Key pieces** could be performed at a private 'group concert' or even at a more formal concert.

The author wishes to thank Graeme Humphrey and Scott Mitchell for many helpful suggestions.

4

Ab major — relative minor is F minor.

Know the Notes!

1 Write the key signature of Ab major:

2 Write out the notes of the scale:

Ab	Bb	C	Db	Eb	F	G	Ab

3 Write out the notes of the arpeggio:

Ab	C	Eb	Ab

Finger Fitness

I octave both hands tog ✓

Aubade

Key piece in A♭ major

Have a go

Compose or improvise your own tune in A♭ major.

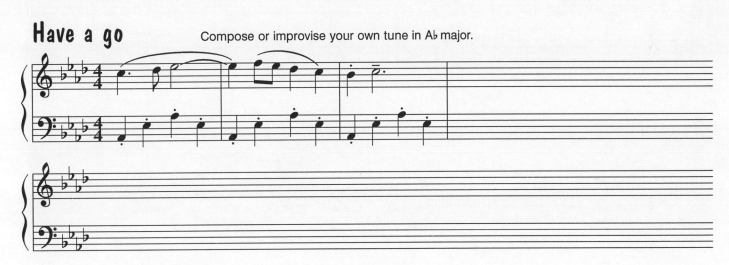

Say Think Play!

Say the notes out loud, up and down.

Think the note names playing the scale or arpeggio very slowly.

Play the scale or arpeggio.

Revision Practice

A♭ major		1	2	3	4	5	6	7	8	9	10
Scale	Rhythmic pattern										
	Dynamic										
Arpeggio	Rhythmic pattern										
	Dynamic										

Marking

A♭ major	Grade
Know the notes!	
Finger fitness	
Key piece	
Have a go	
Say → think → play!	

6

D♭ major

Know the Notes!

1 Write the key signature of D♭ major:

2 Write out the notes of the scale:

| D♭ | E♭ | F | G♭ | A♭ | B♭ | C | D♭ |

3 Write out the notes of the arpeggio:

| D♭ | F | A♭ | D♭ |

Finger Fitness

Practice 1 octave both hands tog.

Dreamy Days   Key piece in D♭ major

Have a go   Compose or improvise your own tune in D♭ major.

Say
Think
Play!

Say the notes out loud, up and down.

Think the note names playing the scale or arpeggio very slowly.

Play the scale or arpeggio.

Revision Practice

D♭ major		1	2	3	4	5	6	7	8	9	10
Scale	Rhythmic pattern										
	Dynamic										
Arpeggio	Rhythmic pattern										
	Dynamic										

Marking

D♭ major	Grade
Know the notes!	
Finger fitness	
Key piece	
Have a go	
Say → think → play!	

B major revision*

*See **Improve your scales!** Piano Grade 3 for more practice material.

Finger Fitness

*use 2, 3 or 4 on this note, at your teacher's discretion

Buttercup

Key piece in B major

Andante espressivo

Revision Practice

	B major	1	2	3	4	5	6	7	8	9	10
Scale	Rhythmic pattern										
	Dynamic										
Arpeggio	Rhythmic pattern										
	Dynamic										

Marking

B major	Grade
Finger fitness	
Key piece	
Say → think → play!	

B♭ major revision*

*See **Improve your scales!** Piano Grade 3 for more practice material.

Finger Fitness

2 octaves.

Butterfly

Key piece in B♭ major

Revision Practice

B♭ major		1	2	3	4	5	6	7	8	9	10
Scale	Rhythmic pattern										
	Dynamic										
Arpeggio	Rhythmic pattern										
	Dynamic										

Marking

B♭ major	Grade
Finger fitness	
Key piece	
Say → think → play!	

E♭ major revision*

*See **Improve your scales!** Piano Grade 3 for more practice material.

Finger Fitness

Energetic Escapade

Key piece in E♭ major

Revision Practice

E♭ major		1	2	3	4	5	6	7	8	9	10
Scale	Rhythmic pattern	✓									
	Dynamic										
Arpeggio	Rhythmic pattern	✓									
	Dynamic										

Marking

E♭ major	Grade
Finger fitness	
Key piece	
Say → think → play!	

C♯ minor

Know the Notes!

1 Write the key signature of C♯ minor:

2 Write out the notes of the harmonic scale:

C#	D#	E	F#	G#	A	B#	C#

3 Write out the notes of the melodic scale:

up→							
C#	D#	E	F#	G#	A#	B#	C#
C#	D#	E	F#	G#	A♮	B♮	←down

4 Write out the notes of the arpeggio:

C#	E	G#	C#

Finger Fitness

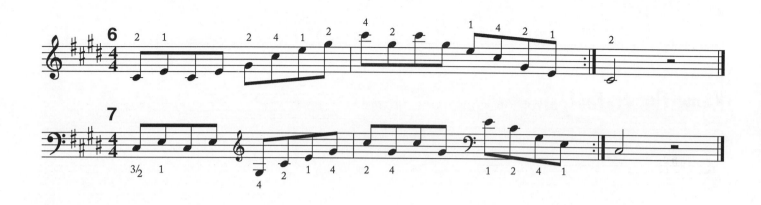

Chimes

Key piece in C# harmonic minor

Contrasts

Key piece in C# melodic minor

Have a go

Compose or improvise your own tune using the notes of C# harmonic minor.

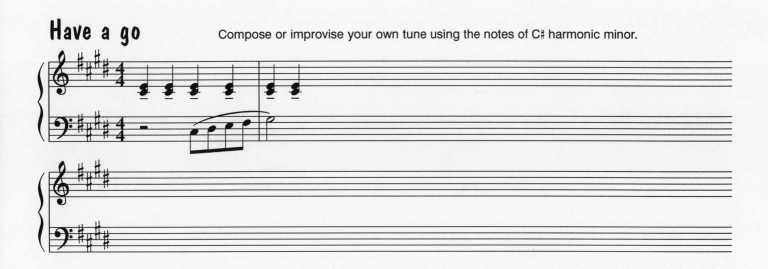

Have another go

Compose or improvise your own tune using the notes of C# melodic minor.

Say Think Play!

Say the notes out loud, up and down.

Think the note names playing the scale or arpeggio very slowly.

Play the scale or arpeggio.

Revision Practice

C# minor		1	2	3	4	5	6	7	8	9	10
Scale	Rhythmic pattern	✓									
	Dynamic										
Arpeggio	Rhythmic pattern										
	Dynamic	✓									

Marking

C# minor	Grade
Know the notes!	
Finger fitness	
Key piece (harmonic)	
Key piece (melodic)	
Have a go	
Have another go	
Say → think → play!	

G# minor

Know the Notes!

1 Write the key signature of G# minor:

2 Write out the notes of the harmonic scale:

G#	A#	B	C#	D#	E	F×	G#

3 Write out the notes of the melodic scale:

up→ G#	A#	B	C#	D#	E#	F×	G#
G#	A#	B	C#	D#	E	F#	←down

4 Write out the notes of the arpeggio:

G#	B	D#	G#

Finger Fitness

*use alternative fingering at your teacher's discretion

Ghostly

Key piece in G♯ harmonic minor

Gossiping

Key piece in G♯ melodic minor

Have a go

Compose or improvise your own tune using the notes of G♯ harmonic minor.

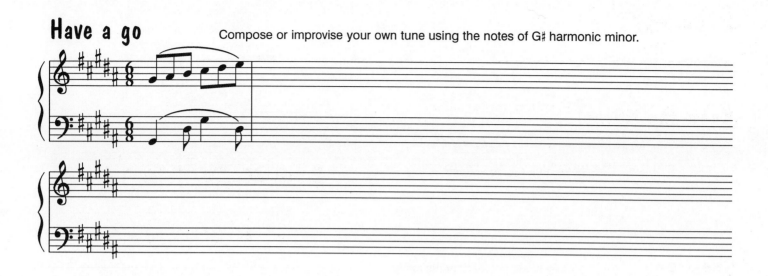

Have another go

Compose or improvise your own tune using the notes of G♯ melodic minor.

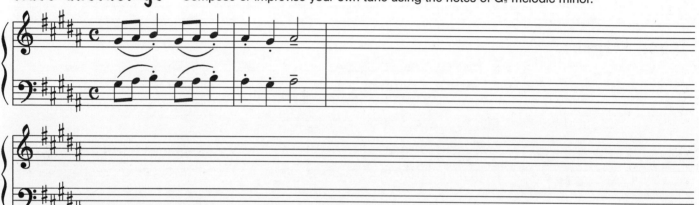

Say Think Play!

Say the notes out loud, up and down.

Think the note names playing the scale or arpeggio very slowly.

Play the scale or arpeggio.

Revision Practice

G♯ minor		1	2	3	4	5	6	7	8	9	10
Scale	Rhythmic pattern	✓									
	Dynamic										
Arpeggio	Rhythmic pattern	✓									
	Dynamic										

Marking

G♯ minor	Grade
Know the notes!	
Finger fitness	
Key piece (harmonic)	
Key piece (melodic)	
Have a go	
Have another go	
Say → think → play!	

F minor

Know the Notes!

1 Write the key signature of F minor:

2 Write out the notes of the harmonic scale:

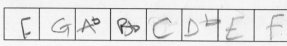

3 Write out the notes of the melodic scale:

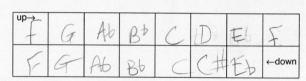

4 Write out the notes of the arpeggio:

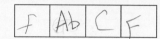

Finger Fitness

Fantasy in Five   Key piece in F harmonic minor

Fiendishly   Key piece in F melodic minor

Have a go

Compose or improvise your own tune using the notes of F harmonic minor.

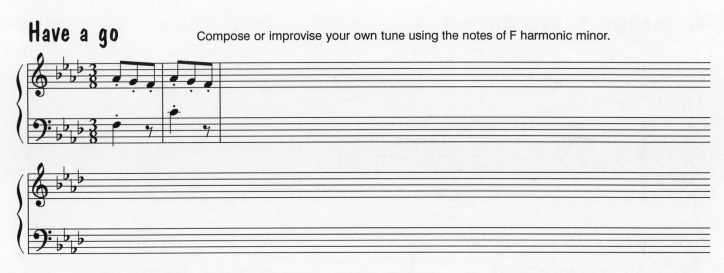

Have another go

Compose or improvise your own tune using the notes of F melodic minor.

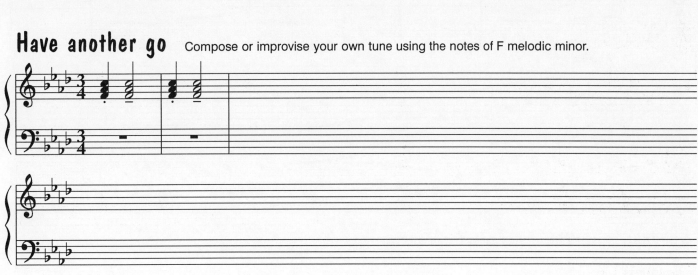

Say Think Play!

Say the notes out loud, up and down.

Think the note names playing the scale or arpeggio very slowly.

Play the scale or arpeggio.

Revision Practice

	F minor	1	2	3	4	5	6	7	8	9	10
Scale	Rhythmic pattern										
	Dynamic										
Arpeggio	Rhythmic pattern										
	Dynamic										

Marking

F minor	Grade
Know the notes!	
Finger fitness	
Key piece (harmonic)	
Key piece (melodic)	
Have a go	
Have another go	
Say → think → play!	

C minor revision*

Finger Fitness

*See **Improve your scales!** Piano Grade 3 for more practice material.

Chrysanthemum   Key piece in C minor

Revision Practice

C minor		1	2	3	4	5	6	7	8	9	10
Scale	Rhythmic pattern										
	Dynamic										
Arpeggio	Rhythmic pattern										
	Dynamic										

Marking

C minor	Grade
Finger fitness	
Key piece	
Say → think → play!	

Arpeggio exercises

In addition to the arpeggios learnt so far, the arpeggios of E, B and F major should be learnt *hands together* as well as hands separately for Grade 4. Practise the following **Finger Fitness** exercises until you can play them with confidence and security.

Revision Practice

key		1	2	3	4	5	6	7	8	9	10
E major	Rhythmic pattern										
	Dynamic										
B major	Rhythmic pattern										
	Dynamic										
F major	Rhythmic pattern										
	Dynamic										

Chromatic scale studies

When practising chromatic scales (hands together) use the following pattern:

Chromatic Crunch
Chromatic study

Contrary motion scale studies

Far apart

Contrary motion scale study in F major

Bagatelle

Contrary motion scale study in B♭ major

Dawn

Contrary motion scale study in D harmonic minor

Grenadiers on Guard   Contrary motion scale study in G harmonic minor

Performance tips

1   Rhythm must be even and the pulse steady throughout – aim for a fluent performance within your technical ability.

2   Tone quality must be as even as possible throughout.

3   Play without accents – listen carefully to passages involving the movement of the thumb.

4   Don't accent the top note.

5   Don't land on the last note with a 'bump'.

6   Don't change tempo or lose rhythmic control when you change direction.

7   At exams, play all scales in the same tempo.

8   Remember that scales are music; play each one with shape and direction.

Scales

SCALES (exam requirements of the Associated Board)
From memory:

Scales: major and minor (melodic *or* harmonic at candidate's choice):
 (i) in similar motion with hands together one octave apart, and with each hand separately, in the following keys:

    B, B♭, E♭, A♭, D♭ majors
    C♯, G♯, C, F minors } (two octaves)

(ii) in contrary motion with both hands beginning and ending on the key-note (unison), in the keys of F and B♭ majors, and D and G *harmonic* minors (two octaves)

Chromatic Scales: in similar motion with hands together one octave apart, and with each hand separately, beginning on any black key named by the examiner (two octaves)

B major 2 octaves

B♭ major 2 octaves
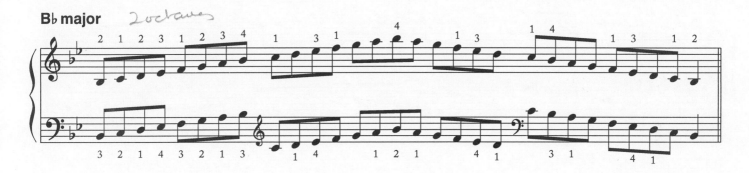

E♭ major 2 octaves
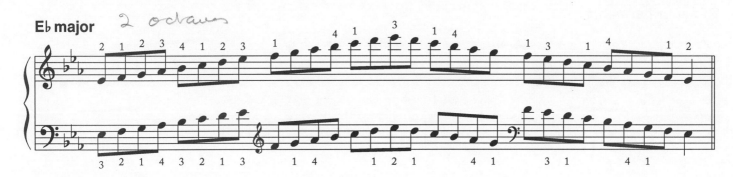

A♭ major 2 octaves.

NEEDS WORK

2 octaves

C minor harmonic

C minor melodic

1 octave.

F minor harmonic

F minor melodic

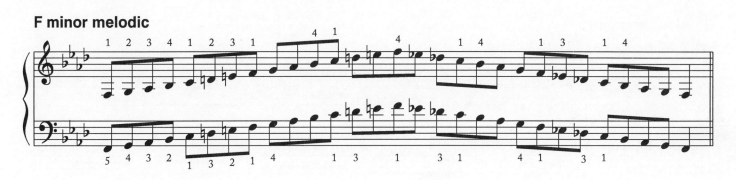

F major contrary motion

B watch
4th finger.

Practice
To here

B♭ major contrary motion

D minor harmonic contrary motion

G minor harmonic contrary motion

Chromatic Scales (hands separately and hands together)

8/7/03

Arpeggios

ARPEGGIOS (exam requirements of the Associated Board)
From memory:

Arpeggios:
(i) the common chords of E, B and F majors, in root position only, in similar motion with hands together one octave apart, and with each hand separately (two octaves)
(ii) the common chords of E♭, A♭ and D♭ majors, and C♯, G♯, C and F minors, in root position only, with each hand separately (two octaves)

Hands separately and hands together:

Hands separately (continued):

Hands separately:

Broken chords

BROKEN CHORDS (exam requirements of the Associated Board)
From memory:

Broken Chords: formed from the chords of Bb major and G minor, with each hand separately, according to *both* Patterns 1 and 2.

Practise broken chords choosing a different rhythm for each practice session.
Mark the rhythm you have chosen in the table.

	1	2	3	4	5	6	7	8	9	10
Bb major (pattern 1)	✓	✓	'							
G minor (pattern 1)	✓	✓								
Bb major (pattern 2)	✓	✓								
G minor (pattern 2)	✓	✓								

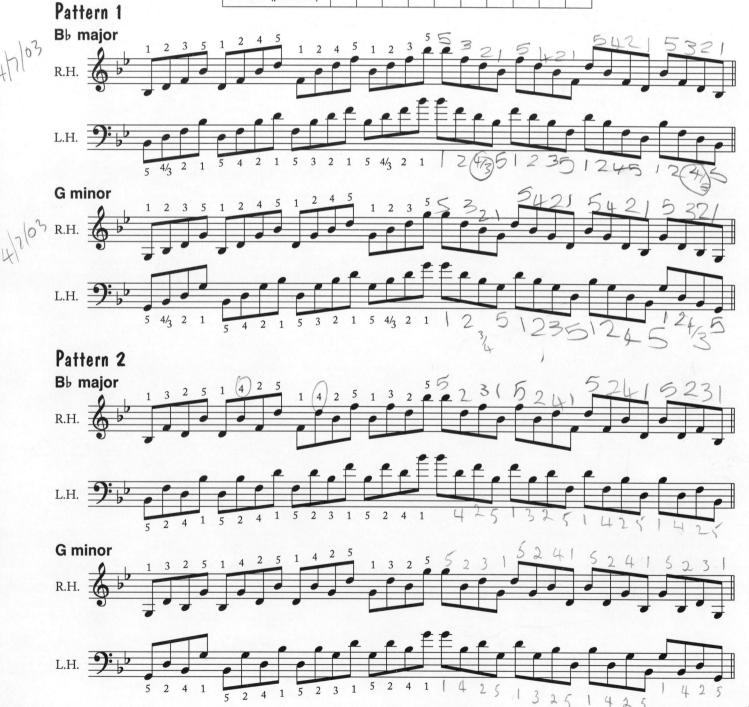

Educational publications from Faber Music

PIANO

Up-Grade! Piano Grades 0-1 *Pamela Wedgwood*

ISBN 0-571-51737-4

More Up-grade! Piano Grades 0-1 *Pamela Wedgwood*

ISBN 0-571-51956-3

Up-Grade! Piano Grades 1-2 *Pamela Wedgwood*

ISBN 0-571-51560-6

Up-Grade! Piano Grades 2-3 *Pamela Wedgwood*

ISBN 0-571-51561-4

Up-Grade! Piano Grades 3-4 *Pamela Wedgwood*

ISBN 0-571-51775-7

Up-Grade! Piano Grades 4-5 *Pamela Wedgwood*

ISBN 0-571-51776-5

The Jazz Piano Master *John Kember*

ISBN 0-571-51791-9

Progressive Jazz Studies. Level 1 *John Kember*

ISBN 0-571-51582-7

Progressive Jazz Studies. Level 2 *John Kember*

ISBN 0-571-51583-5

FABER *ff* MUSIC